TI-92 & CBL Interdisciplinary Activities

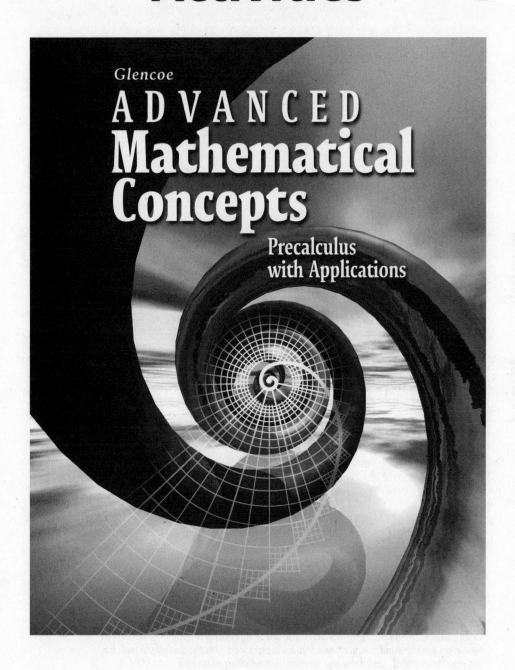

Glencoe
ADVANCED
Mathematical
Concepts
Precalculus
with Applications

Glencoe
McGraw-Hill

New York, New York   Columbus, Ohio   Woodland Hills, California   Peoria, Illinois

Glencoe/McGraw-Hill

A Division of The **McGraw·Hill** Companies

Send all inquiries to:
Glencoe/McGraw-Hill
8787 Orion Place
Columbus, OH 43240-4027

ISBN: 0-07-820387-2   *AMC TI-92 & CBL Interdisciplinary Activities Masters*

7 8 9 10 024 12 11 10 09

Contents

Overview

This booklet contains 12 labs designed to allow students to explore topics in engineering, music, earth science, physics, biology, and chemistry through a stimulating, yet straightforward approach. In each lab, students use the tools of algebra to analyze data they have collected or to explore concepts.

Four labs in this booklet are written for use with the Texas Instruments Calculator-Based Laboratory™ (CBL™) System. The CBL System allows students to gather data, retrieve it directly into a TI-82, TI-83, TI-83 Plus, TI-85, TI-92, or TI-92 Plus calculator, and then analyze the data using the calculator's data modeling and graphing features.

There are four-page labs in this manual. The student portion of each lab is divided into six sections: Introduction, Objectives, Materials, Procedure, Data and Observations, and Analysis.

Introduction explains the science concepts involved in the activity. Specific information necessary for the investigation of the problem is emphasized.

Objectives provides performance objectives for students. Students who do not understand the goal of an activity should benefit from a rereading of the Objectives statements.

Materials is a list of materials for the activity. Most of the labs do not require elaborate supplies or extensive pre-lab preparations. However, you may want to start assembling the required materials a few days before students begin their work on the activity. Students may be able to obtain some of the materials from their homes.

Procedure is the step-by-step instructions for the activity. You may want to discuss the procedure with students before they begin the activity. Pre-activity discussions will help prevent misuse of equipment that can result in damage to the equipment or injuries to students.

Data and Observations includes graphs, charts, and tables to help facilitate data collection and recording. Emphasis should be placed on the need to record all observations during and at the completion of the activity. In many cases, recorded data provide the necessary link between cause-and-effect relationships.

Analysis contains questions requiring students to analyze the data they have collected. In many cases, students will need to use a formula or an equation to perform the necessary calculations. Students should work alone to complete this section, except in activities where group work or class averages are required.

Following the student pages for each lab are two pages of Teaching Suggestions. These pages contain sample data and answers, as well as suggestions for teaching and extending the lab.

Chapter 2

Lab 1 (Use after Lesson 2-5)

Chemistry: Finding Solutions

Chemists and painters, as well as people in many industrial fields, often need to make solutions of a particular strength or concentration. They can either experiment to find the right strength through trial and error, or they can use equations to arrive at the correct concentration the first time.

In this activity, you will use both experimentation and mathematical equations to solve the same problem. You are going to try to match the "concentration" of a certain solution by using color as the indicator of the concentration. First you will try to match the color by mixing different amounts of the original solutions. Then you will solve systems of equations to come up with your mixture.

Objectives

- Find the proper mixture of two solutions to form a third solution.

- Use the TI-92 to find the proper mixture of two solutions to form a third solution.

Materials

- apron
- 30% solution, 80% solution
- 100 mL beakers or other containers (2)
- 200 mL beaker or other clear container

- 10 mL graduated cylinder
- stirring rod or spoon
- TI-92 calculator

Procedure

A. Mixture by Trial and Error

1. Get about 100 mL of each of the two solutions (30% and 80%) from your teacher. Label each mixture. Make sure your 200 mL beaker is clean and dry.

2. Begin your first trial. Using increments of 5 mL and 10 mL, try mixing 100 mL total of the two solutions to make a third solution of 60% (try to match the color sample your teacher has for the class). Keep track of how much of each solution you use. Do not make more than 100 mL of the third solution. Record how much you mixed of each solution in the data table.

3. Repeat Steps 1 and 2 for a second trial. Alter your method and possibly the amounts of solution to achieve a closer color match, but continue using increments of only 5 mL and 10 mL. Record how much you mixed of each solution in the data table.

B. Mixture by Mathematics

4. Write the two equations you will need to solve to find a mathematical solution to this problem. Write these equations in the data table.

5. Now write the equation system as a matrix equation. Write the matrix equation in the data table.

6. Use the TI-92 to solve your matrix equation. Use the *simult* function with a matrix to solve the problem. Write the solution in the data table.

Chapter 2

Lab 1 (continued)

Data and Observations

Data Table

	Amount of 30% solution	Amount of 80% solution	Too light?, Too dark?, Correct color?
Trial 1			
Trial 2			
Trial 3			
The two equations I need to solve are:			
The matrix equation I need to solve is:			
I will need _____ mL of 30% solution and _____ mL of 80% solution.			

Analysis

7. How easy was it to match the color of the third solution using trial and error?

   _____

8. Were three trials more helpful than one trial to find a close color match for the third solution?

   _____

9. What was the mixture amount of your best trial and error that was closest to the mathematical solution?

   _____

10. Refer to the matrix equation you found. What is the inverse of the coefficient matrix?

11. Name at least three disadvantages of using trial and error versus using mathematics to solve this type of problem.

   _____

   _____

Lab 1 Teaching Suggestions

Chemistry: Finding Solutions

Objectives

- Find the proper mixture of two solutions to form a third solution.

- Use the TI-92 to find the proper mixture of two solutions to form a third solution.

Recommended Time

1 class period

Materials

- aprons (40)
- 30% solution, 80% solution (3 L each)
- 60% sample solution (100 mL)
- 10 mL graduated cylinders (10)
- 100 mL beakers or other containers (20)

- 200 mL beakers or other clear containers (10)
- stirring rods or spoons (10)
- TI-92 calculators (10)

Preparation

Prepare the "30% solution" by putting 2 drops of light food coloring (for example, red) per liter of water. Prepare the "80% solution" by putting 1 drop of dark food coloring (for example, blue) per liter of water. Red and blue work well in this activity since, when mixed, they give a good color distinction (red-purple to purple to blue-purple). Prepare one or more samples of "60% solution" by mixing 40 mL of the 30% solution with 60 mL of the 80% solution.

Be sure the room is well lit and has a large white screen or wall so students can compare their solution color.

Teaching the Lab

- Have students work in groups of three or four. Be sure students wear aprons to avoid staining clothes with colored water.

- Point out to students that you are using different colors to represent the different concentrations. (Food coloring is so concentrated that it is very difficult to tell a 60% solution from an 80% solution if the same color dye is used.) Remind students that the purpose of this exercise is to see how mathematics can be used in place of trial and error.

- Remind students to use the white screen or wall to better compare their solution color.

Lab 1 Teaching Suggestions (continued)

Data and Observations

Data Table

	Amount of 30% solution	Amount of 80% solution	Too light?, Too dark?, Correct color?
Trial 1	Answers will vary.	Answers will vary.	Answers will vary.
Trial 2	Answers will vary.	Answers will vary.	Answers will vary.
Trial 3	Answers will vary.	Answers will vary.	Answers will vary.
The two equations I need to solve are:	$x + y = 100$ $3x - 2y = 0$		
The matrix equation I need to solve is:	$\begin{bmatrix} 1 & 1 \\ 3 & -2 \end{bmatrix} \begin{bmatrix} x \\ y \end{bmatrix} = \begin{bmatrix} 100 \\ 0 \end{bmatrix}$ OR $\begin{bmatrix} 3 & -2 \\ 1 & 1 \end{bmatrix} \begin{bmatrix} x \\ y \end{bmatrix} = \begin{bmatrix} 0 \\ 100 \end{bmatrix}$		
I will need ___40___ mL of 30% solution and ___60___ mL of 80% solution.			

Analysis

7. Most students should not have encountered great difficulty in coming close to a match, but may have found it difficult to "fine tune" the color so that it matched exactly.

8. Answers will vary. Most students should find three trials more helpful than 1 trial.

9. Answers will vary. The correct mixture is 40 mL of 30% solution and 60 mL of 80% solution.

10. If the coefficient matrix is $\begin{bmatrix} 1 & 1 \\ 3 & -2 \end{bmatrix}$, the inverse is $-\frac{1}{5}\begin{bmatrix} -2 & -1 \\ -3 & 1 \end{bmatrix}$. If the coefficient matrix is $\begin{bmatrix} 3 & -2 \\ 1 & 1 \end{bmatrix}$, the inverse is $\frac{1}{5}\begin{bmatrix} 1 & 2 \\ -1 & 3 \end{bmatrix}$.

11. Answers will vary. Possible answers include less waste of materials to find correct answer, less expensive to find correct answer, less time to find correct answer, and less precise than using mathematics to find correct answer.

Further Explorations

Solving systems of equations is not limited to making solutions. Students may wish to explore the use of solving systems of equations in a proposed career field, a hobby, or other personal application. Have these students write a paragraph or prepare a sample of how solving systems of equations are used in these fields. Have students mount these displays and post them in the classroom throughout the study of this chapter.

Chapter 3

Lab 2 (Use after Lesson 3-6)

Physics: Pitching a Perfect Parabola

Think about the path of a pop fly ball over a baseball field. As the baseball soars into the sky and then falls to the ground, its path looks like a parabola. Look around, and you'll see parabolas all around you. Even satellite dishes look like parabolas.

Objectives

- Try to make perfect parabola "halves" by throwing a paper ball and following its trajectory.

- Use the TI-92 to plot ideal results for the trials.

- Compare the curve of your paper ball's trajectory with actual parabolic curves.

Materials

- masking tape (approximately 3 meters)
- TI-92 calculator
- graph paper

- sheet of paper, wadded tightly into a ball
- marker
- measuring tape or meterstick

Procedure

A. Pitching a Perfect Parabola

1. Put a 2-meter line of masking tape on the floor, down an aisle of your classroom, or parallel to a wall.

2. As you begin this activity, the path of your paper ball should look similar to the equation $y = -x^2 + 0.5$. Use the TI-92 to make a graph displaying $y = -x^2 + 0.5$. To simulate regular graph paper, set the window to xmin = -10, xmax = 10, ymin = -5, ymax = 5, xscl = 1, and yscl = 1. Copy the graph on a piece of graph paper.

3. Measure a horizontal length of 0.7 meters from the 0 edge of the masking tape. Mark it on the tape using the marker. Then measure a vertical height of 0.5 meters. You may wish to mark the height using masking tape. Stand at the 0 edge of the masking tape. Practice gently throwing the paper ball from that height so that it hits the 0.7 meter mark on the tape on the floor. Note: The wadded paper ball should be thrown horizontally only—not upward or downward. Practice until the mark is hit with reasonable accuracy at least three times, getting a feel for the amount of force that is used to hit the mark. Sketch the path of the ball on the same piece of graph paper.

B. How Perfect is Your Parabola?

4. Measure a vertical height of 1 meter. Throw the paper ball from that height, using the same force that you practiced in the first part of this activity. Measure where the paper ball hits the tape on the floor. Do this three times and average your results. Record your results in the Data Table.

5. Repeat Step 4 for vertical heights of 1.5 meters and 2 meters. Record your results in the Data Table.

Chapter 3

Lab 2 (continued)

Data and Observations

Data Table

Vertical Height	Horizontal Distance	Path of Paper Ball (be sure to label each path)
1 meter		
1.5 meters		
2 meters		

Analysis

6. Compare your observations of the path of the ball in Part A with the equation $y = -x^2 + 0.5$. How close was the path to the actual graph?

   _____

   _____

7. When you are throwing the paper ball from the vertical height, what critical point does the vertical height represent?

8. What three parabolic equations were you trying to imitate in Part B?

   _____

   _____

9. Use the TI-92 to graph the three equations in Exercise B on the same coordinate plane. In your opinion, how close were your results to the actual graphs?

   _____

10. What factors may have kept you from throwing a perfect parabola?

    _____

    _____

6

Lab 2 Teaching Suggestions

Physics: Pitching a Perfect Parabola

Objectives

- Try to make perfect parabola "halves" by throwing a paper ball and following its trajectory.

- Use the TI-92 to plot ideal results for the trials.

- Compare the curve of your paper ball's trajectory with actual parabolic curves.

Recommended Time

1 class period

Materials

- masking tape (approximately 30 meters)
- TI-92 calculators (10)
- graph paper (at least 10 sheets)

- sheets of paper, wadded tightly into a ball (10)
- markers (10)
- measuring tapes or metersticks (10)

Preparation

Have students clear aisles in the classroom before doing this activity. If possible, arrange to perform this experiment in a hallway, where there is substantial room and a nearby wall for students to mark vertical measurements using masking tape.

Teaching the Lab

- Have students work in groups of four. For greater consistency in the results, first have students choose from the following roles.

   Paper ball thrower: Responsible for throwing the paper ball in all trials of the experiment.

   Measurer: Responsible for making measurements and marking the horizontal distance the ball travels.

   Observer: Responsible for watching and recording the path of the paper ball.

   Data recorder: Responsible for recording all data.

7

Data and Observations

Sample Data Table

Vertical Height	Horizontal Distance	Path of Paper Ball (be sure to label each path)
1 meter		
1.5 meters		
2 meters		

Analysis

6. Answers will vary. Most students should find that the path was close to the actual graph.

7. The vertical height represents the critical point: *the maximum.*

8. The three parabolic equations being imitated are the following:

$$y = -x^2 + 1$$
$$y = -x^2 + 1.5$$
$$y = -x^2 + 2$$

9. Answers will vary. Most students should have results that are similar to the actual graphs, provided proper care was used during the activity.

10. Answers will vary. Students should list nonmathematical factors, such as maintaining the proper throwing force, human error in recording the path of the ball, irregularities inherent to using a wadded paper ball, air currents, and so forth.

Further Explorations

Have students test how varying the force they use in throwing a baseball affects the throw. Have students throw the ball from a constant vertical height. (Height should be comfortable for student.) Have students experiment with the throwing force, trying to double the force each time. (Try each throw at least three times, averaging the results.) How does the force of the throw affect the path of the baseball? How would the equation of a parabola reflect this effect?

Chapter 4

Lab 3 (Use after Lesson 4-1)

Physics: "Accelerated" Math

The equation, $d = v_i t + \frac{1}{2}at^2$ is a very useful polynomial with many practical applications. It can be used to tell when an object will hit the ground, how far an object will travel given a certain time and acceleration, and tell the initial speed of an object. In this activity, you will find an object's acceleration down a ramp, and then you will explore how the mass of an object affects its acceleration.

Objectives

- Use the CBL unit and the Vernier Motion Detector to find the acceleration of an object down a ramp.

- Find how mass affects an object's acceleration.

Materials

- toy car or skate
- masking tape
- several washers, quarters, or weights
- CBL unit
- Vernier Motion Detector
- meterstick
- 2-meter-long ramp
- TI-82 calculator

Procedure

A. And Down the Ramp It Goes!

1. Set up the ramp and motion detector as shown above. Use masking tape to make distance marks at 0.5 m, 1 m, 1.5 m, and 2 m. Connect the CBL unit to the TI-82 calculator with the unit-to-unit link cable using the I/O ports located on the bottom edge of each unit. Press the cable ends in firmly. Connect the Vernier Motion Detector to the SONIC port on the left side of the CBL unit. If necessary, obtain the L03ACCL program from your teacher and enter it in the TI-82. Place the motion detector on its side so that the gold foil lies directly on a distance mark and is 0.5 meter away from the path the car will take.

2. Begin the test for $d = 0.5$ meter. Place the car at the top of the ramp. Let the car go. After the graph has been made, on the TI-82, press 2nd [DRAW] 4 to get a vertical line on the screen. Use arrow keys to align this line with the *beginning* of the points that represent the car. The displayed x-value gives you an estimation of the time it took the car to pass the distance mark. Repeat this three more times. Discard your highest and lowest results and average the remaining two. Record the information in the Data Table.

3. Repeat Step 2 for distances of 1 meter, 1.5 meters, and 2 meters. Record the information in the Data Table.

Chapter 4

Lab 3   (continued)

4. Determine the acceleration of the car on the ramp for each trial.

B. Does more mass equal faster speed?

5. Set up the ramp with the distance mark at 1 meter. Set up the motion detector at the 1-meter mark as you did in Part A. Hold the car at the top of the ramp and put your other hand just beyond the 1-meter mark. Release the car and note how it strikes your hand. Record your impression of this force in the Data Table.

6. Divide the washers or weights into two piles. Attach 1 pile to the car. (You may use masking tape to do this.) Judge the additional mass of the car by "weighing" it in your hand. Again, hold the car at the top of the ramp and put your other hand just beyond the 1-meter mark. Release the car, note how it strikes your hand, and record your impression of this force in the Data Table. Rerun the acceleration activity with the modified car for this distance mark. Record your results in the Data Table.

7. Attach the second pile of washers on top of the first washers or to the side of the car. Repeat Step 6 with this newly modified version of the car for the 1-meter mark. Record your results in the Data Table.

8. Determine the acceleration for each modification of the car. Record this information in the Data Table.

Data and Observations

Data Table

Part A

	Time	Acceleration
0.5 meter		
1 meter		
1.5 meter		
2 meters		

Part B

	Force	Time	Acceleration
Car with no washers			
Car with 1 pile of washers			
Car with 2 piles of washers			

Analysis

9. Did the acceleration change throughout Part A? _____

10. In Part B, how did the mass of the car affect the force at which the car hit your hand?

_____

11. In Part B, how did the mass of the car affect the acceleration?

_____

Chapter 4

Lab 3 Teaching Suggestions

Physics: "Accelerated" Math

Objectives

- Use the CBL unit and the Vernier Motion Detector to find the acceleration of an object down a ramp.
- Find how mass affects an object's acceleration.

Recommended Time

1 or 2 class periods. (Use 2 periods if the program L03ACCL must be entered.) If 2 class periods are used, be sure students note how high their ramps are so they can be set up in the same way each class period.

Materials

- toy cars or skates (10)
- masking tape
- several washers, quarters, or weights
- CBL units (10)
- Vernier Motion Detectors (10)
- metersticks (10)
- 2-meter-long ramps (10)
- TI-82 calculator

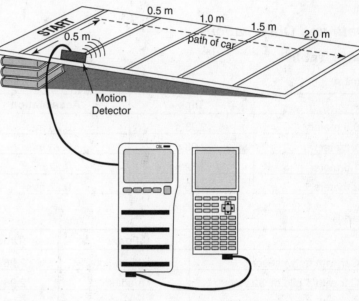

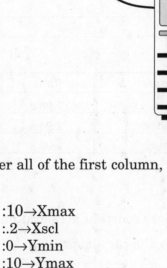

Preparation

Make sure each student group has an open area in which to work.

Use the following program, L03ACCL, for this activity. Enter all of the first column, then the second column, then the third column.

```
PROGRAM:L03ACCL
:Lbl 0
:ClrHome
:Menu("*MAIN
MENU*"),"RUN
ACTIVITY",A,"QUIT",Z)
:Lbl A
:PlotsOff
:Func
:AxesOn
:FnOff
:ClrList L2,L3
:Plot1(Scatter,L2,L3,·)
:0→Xmin
```

```
:10→Xmax
:.2→Xscl
:0→Ymin
:10→Ymax
:.5→Yscl
:60→dim L2
:60→dim L3
:seq(I,I,.1,6,.1)→L2
:{1,0}→L1
:Send(L1)
:{1,11,3}→L1
:Send(L1)
:ClrHome
:Disp "PRESS ENTER"
:Disp "TO START"
```

```
:Disp "ACCL GRAPH."
:Pause
:ClrDraw
:Text(4,1,"DIST")
:Text(51,78,"TIME")
:(3,.1,-1,0)→L1
:Send(L1)
:For(I,1,60,1)
:Get(L3(I))
:Pt-On(L2(I),L3(I))
:End
:Stop
:Goto 0
:Lbl Z
:ClrHome
```

Lab 3   Teaching Suggestions   (continued)

Teaching the Lab

- Have students work in groups of three or four.

- Have students set up their ramps so that the car travels in as close to a straight line as possible.

- Remind students that they should not change the slant of the ramp once they begin this activity.

- Students should be aware that the time expressed using the Motion Detector may not correlate exactly with real time. They should ignore this possible discrepancy and use the time found by the Motion Detector.

- If students use masking tape to attach weights to the car, they should be sure the tape does not interfere with the wheels or catch on the ramp.

Data and Observations

Data Table

Part A

	Time	Acceleration
0.5 meter	2.23 s	0.20 m/s^2
1 meter	2.98 s	0.23 m/s^2
1.5 meter	3.72 s	0.22 m/s^2
2 meters	4.25 s	0.22 m/s^2

Part B

	Force	Time	Acceleration
Car with no washers	medium-light	2.98 s	0.23 m/s^2
Car with 1 pile of washers	medium	2.98 s	0.23 m/s^2
Car with 2 piles of washers	hard	2.98 s	0.23 m/s^2

Analysis

9. Students should find a more or less constant acceleration.

10. The greater the mass, the harder the car struck.

11. The mass of the car should not have affected its acceleration.

Further Explorations

Some students may wish to extend this by testing how fast different objects fall to the ground. For example, in a vacuum, a lead ball and a feather would drop at the same rate and hit the ground at the same time. Dropped off the edge of a table, however, the lead ball will hit the ground first. Students should be able to identify that air friction also enters into this equation when the object is not in a vacuum.

Lab 4 (Use after Lesson 5-4)

Engineering: Mathematics on the Move

You've collected furniture and made some great set pieces and props for a theater production. Now all you have to do is get them to the theater! Since you're smart as well as creative, you decide to use a rolling platform, or dolly, and ramp to move these heavy objects. You know that mathematics involving triangles can be useful in several fields, including engineering. It's a good thing you know a lot about angles and trigonometry to help make moving easier on your muscles!

Objectives

- Use a model to design a useful ramp.
- Use the TI-92 to find out information about your ramp and other "moving" problems.

Materials

- identical books, such as your mathematics textbook (3)
- cardboard "boards" of various lengths
- toy car or other small, wheeled object
- TI-92 calculator
- protractor
- meterstick
- stopwatch or watch with second hand (optional)

Procedure

A. Make a Ramp

1. Use a long, flat surface. Stack your three books at one end of this surface so that they form small steps. Each step should be 2–3 centimeters farther out from the one above it.

2. Select a piece of cardboard. Place the edge of the board against the edge of the top step to simulate a ramp down which you will roll furniture.

3. Place your toy car at the top of the ramp. Hold your hand about 5 centimeters from the bottom of the ramp. Let the car go and record several observations about its path in the Data Table. How quickly did it travel down the ramp? How hard did it hit your hand? Write down any additional notes about the use of this ramp to possibly move boxes and heavy furniture. Keep in mind that in real life, the longer the ramp, the more expensive and heavier it will be.

4. Repeat Steps 2 and 3 with a new ramp. Test five different ramps in all. Test a variety of ramp sizes.

B. Using Brains Along with Brawn

5. Review your notes about your favorite ramp. Knowing the length of the ramp and the length of the side opposite the angle formed by the ramp and the ground, decide which trigonometric function you could use to find the angle of your ramp and the ground. Write the equation in the Data Table. Measure the angle with the protractor. Now use the TI-92 and the angle you measured with the protractor. Using this angle, how close are your actual measurements with what the calculator says?

Data and Observations

Data Table

Ramp Length	Additional Data
Favorite Ramp _____	

Analysis

6. Keep in mind the steepness and length of each ramp. Which ramp would you like to use to move props and heavy furniture with a dolly? Why?

_____

_____

7. What is significant about a ramp whose sin $A = 1$? Assuming this did not bother you, why would it be impossible to use this size ramp in this activity?

_____

_____

8. Think back to the activity. What number will sin A approach if you use increasingly longer ramps? _____

9. Refer to your favorite ramp and the angle you measured with the protractor. Assuming the real steps are a total of 1 meter high, how many meters long would your ramp have to be? Show your work in the form of an equation. Use the TI-92 to solve the equation.

10. Imagine you use a ramp that goes from the top of the steps exactly to the edge of the street. If the angle the ramp makes with the ground is 6° and the horizontal distance from the edge of the street to the top of the steps is 10 meters, how high are the steps? Show your work in the form of an equation. Use the TI-92 to solve the equation.

Chapter 5

Lab 4   Teaching Suggestions

Engineering: Mathematics on the Move

Objectives

- Use a model to design a useful ramp.

- Use the TI-92 to find out information about your ramp and other "moving" problems.

Recommended Time

1 class period

Materials

- identical books, such as the mathematics textbook (30)
- cardboard "boards" of various lengths (approx. 30)
- toy cars or other small, wheeled objects (10)
- TI-92 calculators (10)
- protractors (10)
- metersticks (10)
- stopwatches or watches with second hand (optional—10)

Preparation

Lengths of cardboard should range from 10 cm to 1 meter. (You may wish to vary board length by 5-cm increments) If you do not have time to make the cardboard "boards" of varying lengths, provide students with cardboard and ask each group to make 3 boards. You may wish to assign board lengths to student groups.

Teaching the Lab

- Have students work in groups of three.

- Before students begin the experiment, for greater consistency in the results, have them devise a scale to measure how hard the car hits their hands. They may wish to rank the scale from 1 through 10 with one being "not felt" or "feather-like," and 10 being "struck extremely hard" or "felt like hand was slapped."

Lab 4 Teaching Suggestions (continued)

Data and Observations

Sample Data Table (Data will vary depending on books used and width of steps.)

Ramp Length	Additional Data
0.15 m	Ramp is way too steep—almost straight drop; car crashes at bottom
0.20 m	Ramp is still too steep—car hits bottom too hard
0.35 m	Ramp is somewhat steep—car travels very fast but doesn't crash
0.60 m	Ramp is O.K.—car hits hand with strong but not crushing force (scale 6)
0.90 m	Ramp is O.K.—car hits hand with medium force (scale 4)
Favorite Ramp _____	Data will vary depending on ramp chosen.

Analysis

6. Student answers will vary. Most students will probably want to use a long- to medium-size ramp so that steepness is not too great. Some may take into consideration that the longer the ramp, the more expensive and heavier it will be.

7. The ramp would be vertical. You couldn't use it in this activity because it would not be long enough to cover the steps.

8. zero

9. Answers will vary. Students should use
   tan (measured angle) = 1 meter/length of ramp OR
   cot (measured angle) = length of ramp/1 meter.

10. Students should use
    tan 6° = x meters/10 meters OR
    cot 6° = 10 meters/x meters.
    The steps are approximately 1.05 meters high.

Further Explorations

Have some students use trigonometric functions to describe information about other ramps in their school or community. Have them look at ramps designed for wheelchair access in particular. Have other students explore how trigonometric functions are used in other aspects of engineering. Have them report or demonstrate these techniques to the class.

Chapter 6

Lab 5 (Use after Lesson 6-5)

Music: Rubberband Band

Some people think that music is about as far away from mathematics as one can get. In reality, the opposite is true. Think about a tuning fork. When a tuning fork is struck, it vibrates at a certain speed, making a specific pitch. When a guitar is played, the vibrations of each string produce sounds. Sound waves can be represented as pictured sine curves using an oscilloscope. These representations show what different musical pitches and levels of loudness look like.

Objectives

- Use rubberbands to produce and show different musical pitches and levels of loudness.
- Use the TI-92 to graph different comparisons of sound on the same graph, to better visualize the effects of changes in amplitude (loudness) and period/frequency (pitch).

Materials

- goggles and cotton gloves
- board at least 8 inches wide
- identical, new rubberbands (4)
- 1 inch wide-headed nails (8) and hammer
- $\frac{3}{4}$ inch nails (8) and glue (optional)
- $\frac{1}{2}$ inch wood blocks (8)
- meterstick and marker
- TI-92 calculator

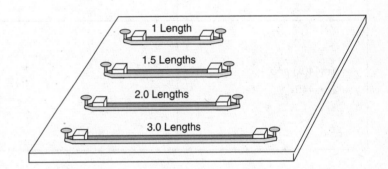

Procedure

A. The Rubberband Band

1. Make a rubberband instrument as shown above. First make your measurements and assemble the board and nails. Pound the nails in so that only $\frac{1}{2}$ inch is showing above the board. Then put the rubberbands on the instrument, pushing them all the way down the nails until they touch the board. Put the small blocks of wood next to the nails between the two halves of the rubberband so that only one strand of the rubberband will vibrate. You may want to nail or glue the blocks to the board—otherwise one student in the group may need to hold them as the rubberband is plucked.

2. Experiment by plucking the rubberbands with your fingertip. How does each rubberband sound compared with the others? What happens when you pluck a rubberband with double your original force? Record your observations in the data table.

B. Music and Mathematics

3. Use the TI-92 to graph some examples of musical sounds. Set the window to $[-3, 3]$ by $[-3, 3]$ with a scale factor of 1 on each axis.

4. A standard in music is the note A above middle C. This A is defined as 440 cycles/sec. Graph $y = \sin(440x)$ on the TI-92. The definition of middle C is 263 cycles/sec. Graph $y = \sin(263x)$ on the TI-92. Show these graphs simultaneously on the same axis. In the data table, make a rough sketch of what you see. Label each graph in your sketch.

5. Now show the two graphs $y = \sin(440x)$ and $y = 2\sin(440x)$ on the TI-92. In the data table, make a rough sketch of what you see. Label each graph in your sketch.

Data and Observations

Data Table

Observations about the Rubberband Instrument	
$y = \sin(440x)$ and $y = \sin(263x)$	
$y = \sin(440x)$ and $y = 2\sin(440x)$	

Analysis

6. How could you expand or "tune" your rubberband instrument so that it plays a more traditional musical scale?

_____

_____

7. What happened to the pitch of the rubberband as the rubberband was stretched to a longer length?

_____

_____

8. What happened to the volume of the rubberband when you plucked it with double the original force?

_____

9. What happens to a musical pitch as the cycles per second (frequency) are increased?

_____

10. When a guitar string is held down at the neck and then plucked, the pitch gets higher. What happens to the string that causes this?

_____

_____

Chapter 6

Lab 5   Teaching Suggestions

Music: Rubberband Band

Objectives

- Use rubberbands to produce and show different musical pitches and levels of loudness.

- Use the TI-92 to graph different comparisons of sound on the same graph, to better visualize the effects of changes in amplitude (loudness) and period/frequency (pitch).

Recommended Time

1 class period (You may need an extra class period if glue is used to stabilize the small wood blocks. In this case the class can make the instrument in one period and perform the activity in the next.)

Materials

- goggles and cotton gloves (for 40 students)
- wood (10 pieces)
- identical, new rubberbands (40—should be medium-sized)
- 1 inch wide-headed nails (80) and hammers (10)
- $\frac{3}{4}$ inch nails (80) and glue (optional)
- $\frac{1}{2}$ inch wood blocks (80)
- metersticks and markers (10)
- TI-92 calculators (10)

Preparation

The wooden boards should be at least 1 inch thick.

Teaching the Lab

- Have students work in groups of four.

- Have students exercise caution when pounding the nails and when stretching the rubberbands over the nails. The cotton gloves should help protect their hands in case a rubberband breaks. Goggles should be worn throughout the activity.

- Measurements for the nails should be: The first rubberband (1) should be stretched slightly over its natural length so that there is some but very little tension. The second rubberband should have a length of $1\frac{1}{2}$ times the length of (1); the third should have a length of 2 times (1), and the fourth should have a length of 3 times (1).

- When students are pounding the nails in, have them leave $\frac{1}{2}$ inch of nail above the board.

Lab 5 Teaching Suggestions (continued)

Data and Observations

Data Table

Observations about the Rubberband Instrument	
$y = \sin(440x)$ and $y = \sin(263x)$	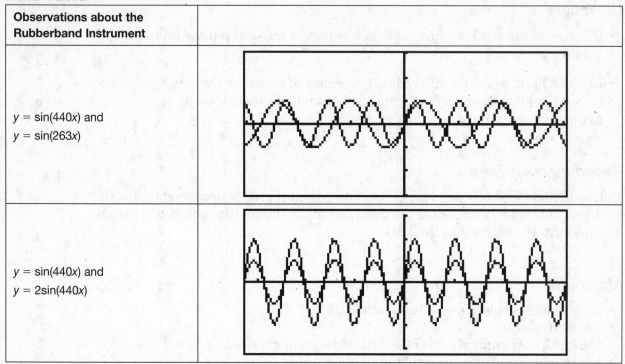
$y = \sin(440x)$ and $y = 2\sin(440x)$	

Analysis

6. Sample answer: The instrument could have more rubberbands added to make the traditional scale, or markings could be made under a small number of rubberbands and the rubberbands held to the board there (similar to a guitar).

7. The pitch became higher.

8. The volume became louder.

9. The pitch becomes higher.

10. Answers will vary. Students should note that the tension of the string does not change, but rather the length of the string is shortened. This is what makes the pitch higher.

Further Explorations

Have interested students demonstrate traditional musical instruments, such as a harpsichord, a flute or recorder, a trumpet, or a guitar or violin. Have them show how different pitches are made on the instrument. You may also wish to make use of the CBL Microphone to show these different pitches and loudness as sound wave patterns. Other students may wish to make a chart showing the eight major musical notes in our scale (rounded to the nearest cycle/sec).

C = 263   G = 392
D = 294   A = 440
E = 330   B = 494
F = 349   C = 524

Advanced Mathematical Concepts

NAME _____ DATE _____ PERIOD _____

Lab 6 (Use after Lesson 7-7)

Physics: Intense Light

You may not think about a lightbulb until it burns out. To change a burned-out lightbulb, people usually remove the lightbulb, check the wattage, and replace it with a new lightbulb of the same wattage. When you turn the light back on, light returns. Just how bright is light?

In this activity, you will measure the intensity of several wattages of white lightbulbs. You will also find out how color affects the lightbulb's intensity.

Objectives

- Use the CBL to measure light intensity for different wattages of white lightbulbs.
- Make a rectangular graph of wattage vs. intensity for the white lightbulbs you tested.
- Compare the intensity of white bulbs with the intensity of a colored bulb by finding the distance from a point to a line.

Materials

- lamp
- white lightbulbs of different wattages (40, 60, 75, 100)
- colored lightbulb
- cotton gloves (1 pair)
- CBL unit with light probe
- TI-82 or TI-83 calculator with unit-to-unit link cable

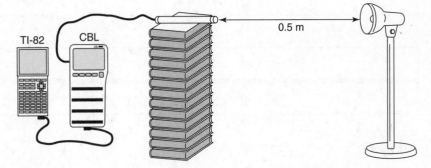

Procedure

A. The Intensity of White

1. Set up your lamp. Balance the light probe on a stack of books 0.5 meter away from your lamp, as shown. The light probe should be on the same level as the widest part of the lightbulb.

2. Set up your CBL system. Use the unit-to-unit link cable to connect the CBL unit to your calculator, using the I/O ports located on the bottom edge of each unit. Connect the end of the light probe to Channel 1 (CH1) on the top edge of the CBL unit. Turn on the CBL unit and the calculator. If necessary, obtain the L06LIGHT program from your teacher and enter it in the calculator.

3. Put on the cotton gloves and keep them on while handling lightbulbs. Put the 40-watt white lightbulb into the lamp. Record the wattage of the bulb in the data table. Turn the light on and take a reading of the intensity of the light given off. Perform four tests in quick succession on the lightbulb. Ignore your highest and lowest readings and average the remaining two. Do not look at the lightbulb while it is on. Record the intensity in the Data Table. Let the lightbulb cool before removing it from the lamp.

4. Repeat Step 3 for each of the white lightbulbs.

5. On a separate piece of graph paper, plot each point (wattage, intensity) using the pairs of values taken from the Data Table. At this distance and at these

Lab 6 (continued)

wattages, the points will be almost linear. Draw a line that has about as many points above the line as below it. The line may contain some of the points. This is your best-fit line.

B. Color Your World

6. Test the colored lightbulb using the same setup as the white lightbulbs. Record the color, wattage, and intensity in the Data Table.

7. Plot the point representing the colored lightbulb on the same graph as the data for the white lightbulbs.

Data and Observations

Data Table

Bulb Color	Wattage	Intensity

Analysis

8. What factors could have interfered with this activity?

_____

9. Refer to your plot of wattage vs. intensity for white lightbulbs. Determine an equation for your best-fit line. Write the equation below.

_____

10. What do you think will happen to light intensity as the lamp is moved farther and farther away from the light probe?

_____

11. Refer to your graph. Find the distance from the point to the line and write it on the graph. Using what you learned in this activity, how could you prove this lightbulb was not white if you looked only at the graph?

_____

_____

12. What do you think a graph of points representing 40-watt, 60-watt, 75-watt, and 100-watt of lightbulbs of the tested color would look like? Describe your hypothesis below.

_____

Chapter 7

Lab 6 Teaching Suggestions

Physics: Intense Light

Objectives

- Use the CBL to measure light intensity for different wattages of white lightbulbs.
- Make a rectangular graph of wattage vs. intensity for the white lightbulbs you tested.
- Compare the intensity of white bulbs with the intensity of a colored bulb by finding the distance from a point to a line.

Recommended Time

1 class period. (An additional class period may be needed if students need to program the TI-82.)

Materials

- lamps (10)
- white lightbulbs of different wattages (40, 60, 75, 100; 10 each)
- cotton gloves (40 pairs)
- TI-82 or TI-83 calculators with unit-to-unit link cable (10)
- light shields (optional; 10)
- colored lightbulbs (10)
- utility clamps (optional; 10)
- ring stands (optional; 10)
- CBL units with light probe (10)

Preparation

Darken the room as much as possible, leaving only a small amount of light. Be sure each group has a clear area that is blocked from other's lamps as much as possible. If lamp shields are necessary, possible suggestions include large boxes with one side removed, cardboard, or curtains. The light shields should extend at least 0.25 meter above the lights.

If a lamp with a shield is not available, another type of lamp may be used.

This activity is best performed using new, unused lightbulbs. NOTE: The lightbulbs must be the same shape and kind. If possible, use a black lightbulb with wattage between 40 watts and 100 watts for this activity. If a black lightbulb is used, caution students to let it cool completely before handling it, as it can get extremely hot. Certain other colors, such as yellow "bug lights," do not offer much contrast with the white lightbulbs. Be sure the colored lightbulb falls within the wattage shown on the graph.

Use the following program, L06LIGHT, for this activity. Enter all of the first column, then the second column, then the third column.

```
PROGRAM:L06LIGHT
:Lbl 0
:ClrHome
:Menu("*MAIN
MENU*"),"RUN
ACTIVITY",A,"QUIT",Z)
:Lbl A
:PlotsOff
:FnOff
:{1,0}→L₁
```

```
:Send(L₁)
:ClrHome
:{1,1,1}→L₁
:Send(L₁)
:ClrHome
:Disp "PRESS ENTER"
:Disp "TO ZERO."
:Pause
:{3,.01,5,0}→L₁
:Send(L₁)
```

```
:ClrHome
:Disp "PRESS ENTER TO"
:Disp "READ
INTENSITY."
:Pause
:(3,.01,5,0)→L₁
:Send(L₁)
:Goto 0
:Stop
:Lbl Z
:ClrHome
```

Lab 6 Teaching Suggestions (continued)

Teaching the Lab

- Have students work in groups of three or four. Each student should take the measurement for at least one test. Each student should record all of the data in his or her data table.

- Remind students not to look at the lightbulb while testing. Remind them to let the lightbulbs cool before handling. Note: a black lightbulb will be especially hot. Students should wear cotton gloves while handling lightbulbs.

Data and Observations

Sample Data Table (Data will vary with distance from light source and lightbulb orientation.

Bulb Color	Wattage	Intensity
White	40	0.838
White	60	0.849
White	75	0.856
White	90	0.860
Black	75	0.830

Analysis

8. Variance in intensity of light from other groups performing the activity, previous usage of lightbulb, aberrations within the lightbulbs, and so forth, could have interfered.

9. The rough equation for this data is $y = 0.00044x + 0.820$. Equations may vary slightly depending on line drawn.

10. As the lamp is moved farther away from the light probe, the light dissipates. The graph of intensity looks more like a curve as the lamp is moved farther away from the light probe.

11. Distance will vary depending on equation and color lightbulb used. Students could prove the lightbulb was not white by showing that the data point is off of the line.

12. Most students should assume that the line will have the same slope as the line for the white lightbulbs and that it will be the determined distance away from the line for the white lightbulbs.

Further Explorations

Interested students may wish to study the intensity of several colors of lightbulbs. They may wish to look at the relative intensity of these lightbulbs (as compared to white lightbulbs) and the effect of colored light on the moods of people. (Research on the effect of colored light on moods can be as informal as doing a survey among friends and classmates about how different colors of lighting affect their moods.) Other students may wish to use a variety of wattages of lightbulbs and distance from the light source so that the intensity of these colored bulbs is similar to the intensity of a white lightbulb. Students can then test the preferences of different-colored/similar-intensity light on people.

Advanced Mathematical Concepts

Lab 7 (Use after Lesson 8-1)

Physics: Pushes, Pulls, and Vectors

Pushes and pulls can be described by vectors. Think about trying to pull something across the ground with the help of a rope. You might pull on the rope so it's parallel to the ground. You might hold the rope up towards your chest while pulling. You might even turn around, put the rope over your shoulder, and tug on it that way. In each case, you are applying some horizontal force on the rope. By analyzing the vector of force you used, you can find out how much horizontal force you applied.

Objectives

- Use the CBL, TI-82, and Vernier student force sensor to measure the force applied in moving an object.

- Graph the force and the direction in which it was applied as a vector.

- Use the TI-92 to measure and analyze the vector's horizontal component.

Materials

- meterstick
- protractor
- masking tape
- book or other light- to medium-weight object
- string
- CBL unit
- Vernier student force sensor with CBL DIN adapter
- TI-82 calculator
- TI-92 calculator

Procedure

A. How Hard (Total) Did You Pull?

1. Connect the CBL unit to the TI-82 calculator with the unit-to-unit link cable using the I/O ports located on the bottom edge of each unit. Press the cable ends in firmly. Connect the Vernier student force sensor to Channel 1 (CH1) on the top edge of the CBL unit. If necessary, calibrate the force probe (see the Vernier student force sensor guide for details). If necessary, obtain the L07FORCE program from your teacher and enter it in the TI-82.

2. Tie one end of the string around the book or other light- to medium-weight object so that it is easy to pull without tipping over. You may have to attach a separate string to two or more points on the object (in order to stabilize your pull) and tie the main string to that separate string. Attach the other end of the string to the Vernier student force sensor.

3. Use masking tape to put two marks on a flat area—a 0 mark and a mark 0.5 m from the 0. Place the book so that the edge with the string is at the 0 mark. Determine an angle of 45° above the horizontal. Hold the string at that angle. Turn the CBL and the TI-82 on. Start the L07FORCE program

on the TI-82. After starting the force graph, begin pulling steadily on the string in the direction of the determined angle. Be sure the force meter forms a right angle with the string. Use a consistent force to pull the book 0.5 m in 5 seconds. Read the constant force on the TI-82. (You will be able to tell when you have reached the constant force when the line on the student force sensor becomes horizontal. You may want to change Ymax and Ymin on the TI-82 to adjust the viewing window.) On the TI-82, press 2nd [DRAW] 3 to get a horizontal line on the screen. Use the arrow keys to align this line with the constant force. The displayed y value gives you an estimation of the average constant force applied during this time. Record this value in the Data Table.

4. Repeat Step 3 for an angle of 30°. Repeat again for an angle of 15° and then for an angle of 0°.

B. How Hard (Horizontally) Did You Pull?

5. Use the TI-92. Draw the vector that represents the force you applied at an angle of 45°. Draw the downward vertical component vector on the same graph, putting the tail of this vector at the head of the initial vector. Compute the horizontal force used. Write this force in the Data Table.

6. Repeat Step 5 for the data at the angles of 30°, 15°, and 0°. Write your results in the Data Table.

Data and Observations

Data Table

	Amount of Force Applied (y-value)	Amount of Horizontal Force Applied
45°		
30°		
15°		
0°		

Analysis

7. Would the horizontal force you apply pulling at a 30° angle be identical to the horizontal force you apply at a –30° angle (pulling down from the horizontal)? Why or why not? Write your answer on a separate piece of paper.

8. Review the total force applied and the horizontal force applied for each angle. What pattern do you see? Write your answer on a separate piece of paper.

9. Review your data. How hard do you think the total force applied would be if the force were applied at 60°? Explain how you got your answer. Write your answer on a separate piece of paper.

10. Would a force applied at 90° produce a horizontal force that is one-half the horizontal force applied at 45°? Why or why not? Write your answer on a separate piece of paper.

Lab 7   Teaching Suggestions

Physics: Pushes, Pulls, and Vectors

Objectives

- Use the CBL, TI-82, and Vernier student force sensor to measure the force applied in moving an object.
- Graph the force and the direction in which it was applied as a vector.
- Use the TI-92 to measure and analyze the vector's horizontal component.

Recommended Time

1 class period (2 class periods will be needed if entering the L07FORCE program.

Materials

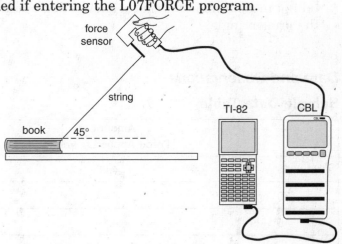

- metersticks (10)
- protractors (10)
- masking tape
- book or other light- to medium-weight objects (10)
- string
- CBL unit
- Vernier student force sensor with CBL DIN adapter
- TI-82 calculators (10)
- TI-92 calculators (10)

Preparation

Use the following program, L07FORCE, for this activity. Enter all of the first column, then the second column, then the third column.

```
PROGRAM:L07FORCE
:Lbl 0
:ClrHome
:Menu("*MAIN
MENU*"),"RUN
ACTIVITY",A,"QUIT",Z)
:Lbl A
:PlotsOff
:FnOff
:AxesOn
:0→Xmin
:99→Xmax
:-5→Ymin
:10→Ymax
:10→Xscl
:2→Yscl
```

```
:ClrList L2,L4
:{1,0}→L1
:Send(L1)
:ClrHome
:{4,1,1,1,9.8,-9.8}→L1
:Send(L1)
:{1,1,1,0,0,1}→L1
:Send(L1)
:Disp "PRESS ENTER"
:Disp "TO START"
:Disp "FORCE GRAPH."
:Pause
:{3,.1,-1,0}→L1
:Send(L1)
:99→dim L4
:ClrDraw
```

```
:Text(4,1,"FORCE(N)")
:Text(51,81,"T(S)")
:For(I,1,99,1)
:Get(L4(I))
:Pt-On(I,L4(I))
:End
:seq(N,N,0,9.8,.1)→L2
:9.8→Xmax
:1→Xscl
:Plot1(Scatter,L2,L4,·)
:DispGraph
:Text(4,1,"FORCE(N)")
:Text(51,81,"T(S)")
:Stop
:Goto 0
:Lbl Z
:ClrHome
```

Lab 7 Teaching Suggestions

Preparation (continued)

Be sure there is a large open area for students to work in. Be sure all groups of students pull the same type and weight object. If the object is much lighter or heavier than a book the window of the TI-82 will have to be adjusted.

Teaching the Lab

- Have students work in groups of three or four.

- You may have students measure the pulling angle by using a protractor or by taking measurements with the meterstick and using trigonometry to compute the proper angle.

Data and Observations

Sample Data Table

	Amount of Force Applied (y-value)	Amount of Horizontal Force Applied
45°	4.68	3.31
30°	4.44	3.86
15°	4.19	4.03
0°	3.95	3.95

Analysis

7. The horizontal force would be the same. Only the direction of the vertical force is changed.

8. Students should see that as pulls are closer to 0°, the force applied is less and is closer to the horizontal force applied.

9. Answers will vary. Students should extrapolate the data to 60°.

10. The force would not be one-half the value. A force applied at 90° would pull an object straight up, and not produce any horizontal force. Students may use data from this activity to also justify this answer.

Further Explorations

A participant in a tug-of-war generally pulls at an angle of 0°. Have interested students explore why it might be easier for a person to move some objects, for example a small wagon, using a 45° pull rather than a 0° pull. They may use the CBL, TI-82, and Vernier student force sensor in this exploration. [It is probably more difficult to move a small wagon by bending over to pull it (with a 0° pull) than it would be to move it by pulling it at waist (approximately 45°) level.]

Lab 8   (Use after Lesson 9-4)

Marine Biology: Polar Sonar

Marine biologists use sonar equipment to track the seasonal migrations and daily movements of fish and whales. The equipment's display panels use polar coordinates to locate the position and trace the motion of the aquatic life forms. In this activity, you will graph the path of a school of fish that marine biologists might study by sonar. Then you will share information with another group of students. You will determine these fish's linear path by using the other group's sonar information.

Objectives

- Determine the linear equation that represents the path of a school of fish.

- Write a polar form of the path and graph it on a polar plane.

- Use the TI-92 to graph a polar equation.

- Write the rectangular form of a polar equation.

Materials

- 2 identical ocean maps
- rectangular-coordinate overlay or ruler
- polar plane graph paper
- TI-92 calculator

Procedure

A. First, Follow the Fish!

1. Obtain 2 identical ocean maps from your teacher. Draw a point to represent an oceanic research ship in the center of both maps. Assume your ship will not be moving. (The point should be in the same place on both maps.) Put one map aside. On the other map, draw a linear path of a group of fish your group will study.

2. Determine the linear equation for the path of your group of fish. To do this, you can either use a rectangular-coordinate overlay or you can use a ruler to draw a rectangular grid on both maps. (If you use a ruler, mark your axes ticks and scale on both maps.) Write the equation in the Data Table.

3. Write the equation for the path of the fish in polar form. Write this equation in the Data Table. Plot this path using a polar plane, similar to what you would see using sonar to track the fish. Include this equation on the polar graph.

4. Exchange the blank ocean map and your polar graph with those of another group of students.

Chapter 9

Lab 8 (continued)

B. Now, Find the Fish!

5. Study the polar graph you got from the other group of students. Look at the polar equation. Use the TI-92 to graph this polar equation on a rectangular grid instead of a polar grid. Sketch this graph in the Data Table.

6. Write the rectangular form of the other group's polar equation. Write this equation on the oceanic map you got from the other group of students and plot the path of the fish.

Data and Observations

Data Table

Your linear equation	
Your polar equation	
TI-92 polar graph for other fish	
How closely did you confirm the data?	

Analysis

7. Compare "research notes" with the other group of students. Did you confirm each other's data?

8. Throughout this activity, you are assuming that the oceanic research ship remains in one place. Explain why this assumption was made.

_____

9. Compare the graph you made on the TI-92 with the linear graph of the fish's path. How are these two graphs similar? How are they different?

_____

Lab 8 Teaching Suggestions

Marine Biology: Polar Sonar

Objectives

- Determine the linear equation that represents the path of a school of fish.
- Write a polar form of the path and graph it on a polar plane.
- Use the TI-92 to graph a polar equation.
- Write the rectangular form of a polar equation.

Recommended Time

1 class period

Materials

- 2 identical ocean maps for 10 groups (photocopied, 20 maps total)
- rectangular-coordinate overlays or rulers (10)
- polar plane graph paper (at least 10 sheets)
- TI-92 calculators (10)

Preparation

It is best to prepare 10 different ocean maps so students do not exchange maps of the same area. You may prepare the maps by photocopying areas of the oceans from an atlas. You may wish to photocopy areas that contain known migration routes of marine animals (eels—North Atlantic Ocean; salmon—North Atlantic Ocean, North Pacific Ocean; tuna—Mid Pacific Ocean; turtles—Mid Atlantic Ocean; whales—Atlantic, Indian, and Pacific Oceans [along the east and west coasts of several continents])

Teaching the Lab

- Have students work in groups of three or four.
- Note that the TI-92 cannot display a polar plane (circular grid).
- Remind students that scientists often take measurements and find data using one form of measurement that is more precise for scientists and then have to interpret their results in "language" that the public understands.

Lab 8 Teaching Suggestions (continued)

Data and Observations

Data Table

Your linear equation	Answers will vary.
Your polar equation	Answers will vary.
TI-92 polar graph for other fish	Answers will vary.
How closely did you confirm the data?	Most students should find their data mirrors very closely.

Analysis

7. Most groups should be able to confirm the data.

8. You are assumed the oceanic research ship remained in one place so you did not have to factor in its movement. Otherwise, the "center point" would keep moving, altering the graph.

9. The graphs are identical.

Further Explorations

Some students may be interested to find out more about how polar coordinates are used in other fields or find out more about how polar coordinates are used in marine biology. Have these students present their information to the class as part of the review for this chapter.

Biology: Using 3-Dimensional Models

Think about going to a movie and seeing a computer-generated sequence that involves 3-dimensional modeling. It looks great on the screen and has a high entertainment value, but is that all there is to it? Computer-generated 3-dimensional modeling has a wide range of exciting applications, especially in the biological sciences. One of these applications is the use of this type of modeling as a learning tool for students. For example, many anatomical models are available for the computer. You can turn and examine these models using the computer instead of sacrificing an animal or learning from a flat page in a book. To get a better feel for how 3-dimensional modeling can be used, you will cut apart a model of a cone in order to better see how geometric figures can be derived. Then you will use the TI-92 calculator to view a 3-dimensional figure from different directions.

Objectives

- Create three geometric figures by cutting a 3-dimensional cone.
- Use the TI-92 to view a 3-dimensional figure from different angles.

Materials

- funnel and wax paper or three cone-shaped paper cups
- modeling clay
- plastic knife
- TI-92 calculator

Procedure

A. Cutting Cones

1. Obtain a funnel lined with wax paper or a cone-shaped paper cup. Fill this mold with modeling clay to make a clay cone. Make 3 identical cones.

2. Choose three of the figures to model.

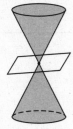
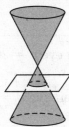
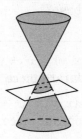
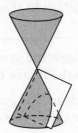
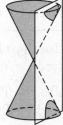

| point (degenerate ellipse) | circle | ellipse | parabola | hyperbola |

3. Using your knife, carefully cut one of your cones into two pieces so that one of your three figures is represented. Draw both of the pieces in the Data Table.

4. Repeat Step 3 with each of the remaining cones. Draw your results in the Data Table.

Lab 9 (continued)

B. More on 3-Dimentional Viewing

5. A 3-dimensional model, like the cone you just used, can be turned and viewed from different directions. Computer-generated models can also be turned and viewed from different directions. Using your TI-92 calculator, enter the paraboloid $z(x, y) = x^2 + y^2$ (an example of this figure is given in the TI-92 Guidebook). Display a 3-dimensional graph of this figure.

6. Experiment using the Window variables (eye$\theta°$ and eye$\phi°$) to view the paraboloid from different directions. Experiment by changing only one variable at a time.

Data and Observations

Data Table

Figure 1	Figure 2	Figure 3

Analysis

7. Think about the graphic representations of the figures you made. How closely do your figures match these graphic representations?

_____

_____

8. What figure would you get if you cut a cone perpendicular to its base through its vertex?

_____

9. You want to cut a cone so that a circle is formed. How should the plane of your cut lie in relation to the cone's base?

_____

10. Use the TI-92 to draw the graph of $z(x, y) = x^2 + y^2$ when eye$\theta° = 20$ and eye$\phi° = 70$. Draw the figure on a separate piece of paper.

11. Use the TI-92 to draw the graph of $z(x, y) = x^2 + y^2$ when eye$\theta° = 20$ and eye$\phi° = 90$. Draw the figure on a separate piece of paper.

12. Compare the following two graphs: $z(x, y) = x^2 + y^2$ when eye$\theta° = 0$ and eye$\phi° = 70$ and when eye$\theta° = 90$ and eye$\phi° = 70$. What does this tell you about this paraboloid and this viewing angle?

_____

_____

Chapter 10

Lab 9 Teaching Suggestions

Biology: Using 3-Dimensional Models

Objectives

- Create three geometric figures by cutting a 3-dimensional cone.

- Use the TI-92 to view a 3-dimensional figure from different angles.

Recommended Time

1 class period

Materials

- funnels (10) and wax paper or cone-shaped paper cups (30)
- modeling clay
- plastic knifes (10)
- TI-92 calculators (10)

Preparation

Have students work in groups of three. Caution students to be very careful when cutting the modeling clay. If using a funnel instead of a cone-shaped paper cup, be sure wax paper lining is positioned so that the molded cone comes out with a point at the top.

Teaching the Lab

- Have students work in groups of three.

- Caution students to use care when cutting the modeling clay.

- If students have difficulty with 3-dimensional graphing with the TI-92, you can refer them to the TI-92 Guidebook.

Data and Observations

Data Table

Figure 1	Figure 2	Figure 3	Figure 4	Figure 5
point	circle	ellipse	parabola	hyperbola

Analysis

7. Student answers will vary. If care was taken, most students should have figures that match the graphic representations.

8. If you cut a cone perpendicular to its base through its vertex, you would get a triangle.

9. The plane of your cut should lie parallel to the cone's base.

10. $z(x, y) = x^2 + y^2$ when eye$\theta° = 20$ and eye$\phi° = 70$

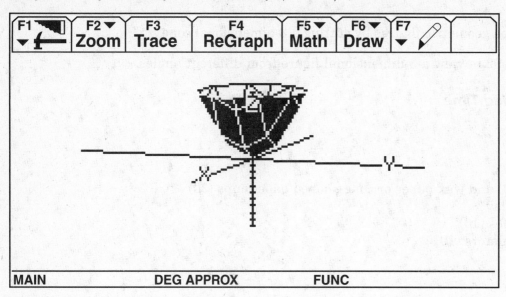

11. $z(x, y) = x^2 + y^2$ when eye$\theta° = 20$ and eye$\phi° = 90$

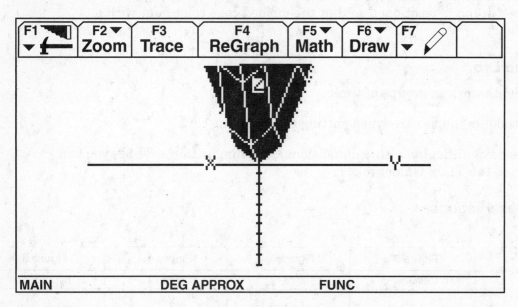

12. This tells you that the paraboloid is symmetrical when viewed around the x-axis.

Further Explorations

Some students may enjoy finding out how 3-dimensional modeling is used in other fields. Have them collect information and photos. Display these presentations in the classroom throughout the remainder of this chapter. Other students may enjoy working with the TI-92 to create 3-dimensional graphs. Allow these students to experiment with different formulas.

Lab 10 (Use after Lesson 11-5)

Chemistry: Hydrogen Ions in Solution

The pH scale is a number scale used to describe the concentration of hydrogen ions (H^+) in a solution. A solution's pH is found using the formula $pH = \log \frac{1}{H^+}$.
A pH of 7 means the solution is *neutral*. Pure water, or H_2O, has as many hydrogen ions as hydroxide (OH^-) in solution. This makes pure water neutral. Values below 7 on the pH scale indicate *acids*, or solutions that contain more hydrogen ions than hydroxide ions. Values above 7 on the pH scale indicate *bases*, or solutions that contain more hydroxide ions than hydrogen ions.

Objectives

- Use litmus paper to determine if a solution is an acid or a base.

- Use the Calculator-Based Laboratory System (CBL) to measure pH.

- Use pH values to determine the concentration of hydrogen ions in a variety of solutions.

- Identify unknown solutions based on the concentration of hydrogen ions.

Materials

- solutions in containers (4)
- red litmus paper (4)
- blue litmus paper (4)
- TI-82 CBL graphics calculator with unit-to-unit link cable
- Vernier pH probe (PHA-DIN amplifier and 7120B electrode) with CBL DIN adapter (not included in the CBL unit)

- distilled water
- masking tape and marker
- ring stand

- utility clamp
- forceps

Procedure

A. More H^+ Ions or More OH^- Ions?

1. Get sample solutions from your teacher. Label the samples 1 through 4.

2. Test the first solution with red litmus paper. Use a forceps to hold a strip of red litmus paper. Dip the paper into the solution, then remove it. (If the forceps touch the sample, wash the forceps in tap water and dry before using them again.) Use the information in Table 1 to classify the solution as an acid or a base. Record the results of your tests in the data table.

3. Repeat Step 2 for each solution. Use a new strip of litmus paper for each solution. Discard the used litmus paper in a container provided by your teacher.

Table 1   Litmus Tests

Color Before Test	Color After Test	Type of Solution	Ions in Greater Numbers
Red	Red	Acid or Neutral	same or more H^+ than OH^-
	Blue	Base	more OH^- than H^+
Blue	Red	Acid	more H^+ than OH^-
	Blue	Base or Neutral	same or more OH^- than H^+

4. Repeat Steps 2 and 3 using blue litmus paper.

Chapter 11

Lab 10   (continued)

B. Measuring pH

5. If necessary, obtain the L10PH program from your teacher and enter it in the TI-82. Set up your CBL system. Use the unit-to-unit link cable to connect the CBL unit to your calculator. Use the I/O ports located on the bottom edge of each unit.

6. Use a utility clamp to attach the pH probe to a ring stand. Connect the other end of the pH probe to the PHA-DIN amplifier and CBL DIN adapter. Plug the assembly into Channel 1 (CH1) on the top edge of the CBL unit. Turn on the CBL unit and the calculator.

7. Place the probe in Sample 1 and let it sit in solution for 5 minutes. Start the L10PH program and take the pH reading. Record the reading in the Data Table. Rinse the probe well with distilled water and let it drip dry for a few seconds.

8. Repeat Step 7 for each sample. Record your readings in the Data Table.

9. Use the pH values in your table and the TI-82 calculator to determine the concentration of hydrogen ions in each sample. Use the equation $pH = \log \frac{1}{H^+}$, where H^+ is the number of gram atoms of hydrogen ions per liter. Record your answers in the data table.

10. The samples you tested are among the solutions listed below. Use the information below to identify the substances according to their concentration of hydrogen ions. Record your answers in the Data Table.

Solution	H^+ Concentration	Solution	H^+ Concentration
lime juice	1.25893×10^{-2}	bottled drinking water	6.30957×10^{-8}
apple juice	1.58489×10^{-4}	milk of magnesia	5.01187×10^{-11}
shampoo	3.16228×10^{-6}	ammonia	1×10^{-11}
milk	3.98107×10^{-7}	household bleach	1.58489×10^{-13}

Data and Observations

Data Table

Sample	Result of Litmus Test	pH Value	H^+ Concentration (gram atoms per liter)	Substance
Sample 1				
Sample 2				
Sample 3				
Sample 4				

Analysis

11. Using the procedure in Part A, can you determine the *concentration* of hydrogen ions? Explain. _____

12. Which sample had the highest concentration of hydrogen ions? _____

13. Which sample had the lowest concentration of hydrogen ions? _____

14. Do you think pH is useful as a tool for identifying an unknown substance? Explain.
_____

Chapter 11

Lab 10   Teaching Suggestions

Chemistry: Hydrogen Ions in Solution

Objectives

- Use litmus paper to determine if a solution is an acid or a base.

- Use the Calculator-Based Laboratory System (CBL) to measure pH.

- Use pH values to determine the concentration of hydrogen ions in a variety of solutions.

- Identify unknown solutions based on the concentration of hydrogen ions.

Recommended Time

- 2 class periods (Students can set up the CBL system and enter the L10PH program in one class period and do the experiment in the next.)

Materials

- solutions in containers (40)
- red litmus paper (40)
- blue litmus paper (40)
- TI-82 CBL graphics calculators with unit-to-unit link cable (10)
- Vernier pH probes (PHA-DIN amplifier and 7120B electrode) with CBL DIN adapters (not included in the CBL unit) (10)
- distilled water
- masking tape and markers (10)
- ring stands (10)
- utility clamps (10)
- forceps

Preparation

Gather sample solutions, choosing bottled drinking water and three other solutions listed in Table 2. Be sure to have at least one acid and one base. Sample data is for fresh lime juice, apple juice, bottled drinking water, and milk of magnesia.

To make the activity more interesting, use containers that will disguise the sample. For example, dark 35-mm film canisters with a hole large enough for the probe in the cover or beakers covered with dark paper with a hole in the top for the probe will help keep students from identifying the samples based on sight.

Use the following program, L10PH, for this activity. Enter all of the first column, then the second column, then the third column.

```
PROGRAM:L10PH                :{4,1,1,1,14.292,-4.17}→L1    :Disp "PRESS TRIGGER"
:Lbl 0                       :Send(L1)                     :Disp "TO COLLECT"
:ClrHome                     :{1,1,1,0,0,1}→L1             :Disp "PH READINGS."
:Menu("*MAIN                 :Send(L1)                     :For(I,1,C,1)
MENU*","RUN                  :Disp "ENTER NUMBER"          :Get(L4(I))
ACTIVITY",A,"QUIT",Z)        :Disp "OF SAMPLES"            :Goto 0
:Lbl A                       :Input C                      :Stop
:ClrList L4                  :C→dim L4                     :Lbl Z
:ClrHome                     :ClrHome                      :ClrHome
:{1,0}→L1                    :{3,0,-1,6}→L1
:Send(L1)                    :Send(L1)
```

Lab 10 Teaching Suggestions (continued)

Teaching the Lab

• Have students work in groups of four. Each student can test one solution. Each student should record data in his or her data table.

• Advise students not to smell the samples, both for safety reasons and to keep them from using smell as an identifying factor.

• Remind students that the number of samples entered into the program is always 1.

• The pH for sample solutions may vary slightly with each reading. Chosen substances differ enough in pH so this is not a factor in identifying the sample.

Data and Observations

Sample Data Table

Sample	Result of Litmus Test	pH Value	H^+ Concentration (gram atoms per liter)	Substance
Sample 1	acid	1.9	1.25893×10^{-2}	fresh lime juice
Sample 2	acid	3.8	1.58489×10^{-4}	apple juice
Sample 3	neutral	7.2	6.30957×10^{-8}	bottled drinking water
Sample 4	base	10.3	5.01187×10^{-11}	milk of magnesia

Analysis

11. Students should recognize that the litmus test is not quantitative and that although they can tell whether a solution is an acid, neutral, or base; if the solution is an acid or base, they will not be able to determine the concentration of hydrogen ions.

12. Answers will vary depending on sample solutions.

13. Answers will vary depending on sample solutions.

14. Students should recognize that pH is an adequate tool for eliminating possible substances. For instance, a substance with pH 8 is unlikely to be vinegar. However, they should also recognize that many solutions can have the same concentration of hydrogen ions, making pH alone not sufficient for substance identification.

Further Explorations

Provide students with information showing that a low concentration of hydrogen ions can be harmful to some living organisms or have students research this information. Have them evaluate the tap water and rain water in your area.

Chapter 12

Lab 11 (Use after Lesson 12-8)

Earth Science: Fractal Geometry vs. Fractal Geography

One of the interesting points about fractal geometry is how often it is represented in nature. Even Benoit Mandelbrot, the "father" of fractal geometry, referred to the "geometry of nature." One aspect of fractal geometry is that curves commonly found in nature, such as coastlines, can be broken down to increasingly smaller parts, depending on the length of measurement used. You will explore this area of fractal geometry by looking at coastlines.

Objectives

- Realize that the "length" of an irregular curve increases as the unit of measurement used to measure the curve decreases.

- Use the TI-92 to show the curvature of coastline data.

- Compare graphs of different countries' coastlines to further investigate coastline data.

Materials

- enlarged, photocopied map
- thin cardboard strips in five lengths
- TI-92 calculator
- graph paper

Procedure

A. The Smaller They Get...

1. Obtain a map of an island. Choose one coastal city or point of the coastline as your starting point.

2. Use the longest cardboard strip (L1). Begin at your starting point. Measure the coastline using L1. Ignore the last segment if it is only a partial measurement. Record your data in the Data Table.

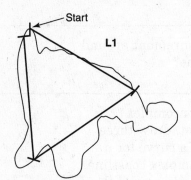

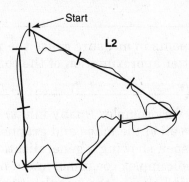

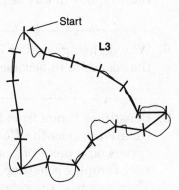

3. Repeat Step 2 for each of the increasingly shorter cardboard strips (L2, L3, L4, and L5). Record your data in the Data Table.

Chapter 12

Lab 11 (continued)

B. ...The Bigger They Are?

4. Use the TI-92 to graph your data. Use x-coordinates of 16 for L1, 8 for L2, 4 for L3, 2 for L4, and 1 for L5. Change your window parameters to xmin = 0, xmax = 20, xscl = 2, ymin = 0, ymax = 200, and yscl = 20. Sketch your graph in the Data Table.

5. Graph your data on a separate piece of graph paper.

6. Post your map and the graph at the front of the class.

Data and Observations

Data Table

Island _____

Measurement Tool	Number of Segments	Graph
L1		
L2		
L3		
L4		
L5		

Analysis

7. If you used a measuring tool that was the length of the longest span of the country, how many segments would you measure?

_____

8. Why do using smaller increments in measure cause the measurement around the coastline to become a better approximation of the coastline?

_____

9. Coastlines range from being very complex (many inlets) to noncomplex (relatively smooth). Compare all of the maps and graphs. First, draw three curves on a piece of graph paper, showing a generalization of a curve for a very complex coastline, a semicomplex coastline, and a noncomplex coastline. Then describe the relationship between the complexity of coastlines and their graphs in terms of how the graphs approach the x-axis.

_____

_____

_____

Lab 11   Teaching Suggestions

Fractal Geometry vs. Fractal Geography

Objectives

- Realize that the "length" of an irregular curve increases as the unit of measurement used to measure the curve decreases.

- Use the TI-92 to show the curvature of coastline data.

- Compare graphs of different countries' coastlines to further investigate coastline data.

Recommended Time

1 class period

Materials

- enlarged, photocopied maps from an atlas (10)
- thin cardboard strips in five lengths (10 each)
- TI-92 calculators (10)
- graph paper(at least 10 sheets)

Preparation

When choosing maps, select a variety of island shapes concerning the complexity, or "brokenness," of the coastlines. Possible islands to choose are: Cuba, Greenland, Honshu of Japan, Iceland, Java of Indonesia, Madagascar, Prince Edward Island, Puerto Rico, Sicily, the United Kingdom, or one of the Hawaiian or Aleutian Islands. Then look at the size of the maps. Choose the length of the first set of cardboard strips so that each group of students will make at least three measurements with it. Each measuring strip should be one-half the size of the previous one.

Teaching the Lab

- Remind students to ignore the last measurement if it is not a whole measurement.

Chapter 12

Lab 11 Teaching Suggestions (continued)

Data and Observations

Sample Data Table

Island _____ Japan _____

Measurement Tool	Number of Segments	Graph
L1	6	
L2	18	
L3	40	
L4	96	
L5	190	

Analysis

7. Two

8. As the increments get smaller, the coastline can be followed more accurately.

9. The graphs should look similar to those shown below. The more complex the coastline is, the slower it approaches the x-axis.

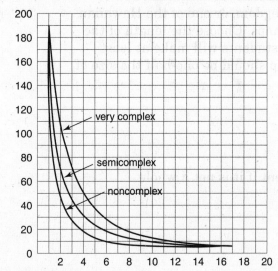

Further Explorations

Have interested students investigate Koch's "island" (snowflake). Have them apply this case to a real snowflake or other crystal.

Chapter 14

Lab 12 (Use after Lesson 14-3)

Biology: Frequency Distribution of a Trait

Organisms exhibit specific characteristics that may identify them as belonging to one species rather than another. However, there are usually variations of the traits present in any species. For example, all sunflowers are composite flowers—they have brown disk flowers surrounded by yellow ray flowers. However, some flowers may be wider than others and some plants may be taller than others. The physical characteristics of sunflower seeds also vary. Mathematics can help clarify some of these characteristics and their variations and help make data easier to understand.

Objectives

- Measure the length of a selection of striped sunflower seeds.

- Use the TI-92 to create a histogram and box-and-whisker plot for the length of sunflower seeds.

Materials

- sunflower seeds
- Vernier caliper or mm ruler
- TI-92 calculator

Procedure

A. One Tiny Seed . . .

1. Look over the selection of sunflower seeds. Estimate the length of the longest and shortest seeds.

2. Make a table of millimeter measurements which allows for tallies of every length of seed from the shortest to the longest.

3. Measure and tally the sample of seeds.

B. Making Sense of the Data

4. Use the TI-92 to create a histogram of your data. Set the window parameters to xmin = 0, xmax = 2.0, xscl = .1, and ymax to half the total number of seeds measured. Set the bar (bucket) width to .1. Copy your histogram on a separate piece of paper. Then create a box-and-whisker plot for the data. Copy this plot on a separate piece of paper.

5. Compile a class tally list on the chalkboard or copy your tally and exchange results throughout the class. Create a tally sheet that reflects the data gathered by all the groups.

6. Use the TI-92 to create a histogram and box-and-whisker plot for the class data. Copy these on a separate piece of paper.

Data and Observations

Data Tables

Group Data	Tally	Frequency *f*

Class Data	Tally	Frequency *f*

Analysis

7. Use your sample to predict what size(s) of seed occurs most frequently. How representative do you think your data will be compared to the compiled data from the rest of your class?

   _____

8. What was the actual range of the data found by the class? _____

9. What was the median of the data found by the class? _____

10. Based on the histogram, would you say that sunflower seeds have a range of sizes or tend to be a certain length? _____

11. Which type of graph is more helpful in telling you about this data? Explain.

   _____

   _____

   _____

Chapter
14

Lab 12   Teaching Suggestions

Biology: Frequency Distribution of a Trait

Objectives

- Measure the length of a selection of striped sunflower seeds.

- Use the TI-92 to create a histogram and box-and-whisker plot for the length of sunflower seeds.

Recommended Time

- 2 class periods (Students can collect the data in one period and complete the graphing in the second period.)

Materials

- sunflower seeds ($\frac{1}{2}$ to 1 pound, striped)
- Vernier calipers or mm rulers (10)
- TI-92 calculators (10)

Preparation

- For best variety, use sunflower seeds from a bulk container, rather than packaged, fancy seeds. Data may vary depending on type of seeds used.

- Prepare approximately equal amounts of seeds for each group in the class. You may wish to give each group approximately 20 seeds.

Teaching the Lab

- Have students work in groups of two or three. Each member of the group should measure some seeds.

Data and Observations

Sample Data Tables

Group Data	Tally	Frequency *f*
1.0 mm	/	1
1.1 mm	/	1
1.2 mm	///// ///// /	11
1.3 mm	//	2
1.4 mm	///	3
1.5 mm	/	1
1.6 mm		0
1.7 mm	/	1

Lab 12 Teaching Suggestions (continued)

Data and Observations (continued)

Class Data	Tally	Frequency *f*
1.0 mm	/////	5
1.1 mm	///// ///// /	11
1.2 mm	///// ///// ///// ///// ///// ///// ///// ///// ///	43
1.3 mm	///// ///// ///// ///// ///	23
1.4 mm	///// ///// //	12
1.5 mm	///// /	6
1.6 mm	/////	5
1.7 mm	///	3

Analysis

7. Most students should feel the sample is large enough to yield data that is fairly representative of the compiled data from the rest of the class.

8. The range was (approximately) 0.7.

9. The median was (approximately) 1.2.

10. The seeds tend to be a certain length—approximately 1.2 to 1.3 millimeters.

11. Most students will probably find the histogram more helpful in this case.

Further Explorations

Later in this chapter, you may wish to have students use the data compiled by the class to explore other forms of data analysis, such as making a frequency polygon and looking at distribution data.